SRA Open Court

Professional Development Guide

Vocabulary

Author

Marsha Roit

A Division of The McGraw-Hill Companies

Columbus, Ohio

Photo Credits:

p. 3, ©Will Hart/PhotoEdit; **p. 6,** ©Charles Gupton/Stock Boston/PictureQuest; **p. 7,** ©Robert E. Daemmrich/Tony Stone Images; **p. 11,** ©Richard Orton/Index Stock; **p. 17,** ©David Young-Wolff/PhotoEdit.

www.sra4kids.com

SRA/McGraw-Hill

A Division of The ***McGraw·Hill*** *Companies*

Send all inquiries to:
SRA/McGraw-Hill
8787 Orion Place
Columbus, Ohio 43240-4027

Printed in the United States of America.

ISBN 0-07-571266-0

1 2 3 4 5 6 7 8 9 MAL 05 04 03 02 01

Table of Contents

Vocabulary

Our lives, personal and professional, are dominated by words—the words we speak and hear and the words we read and write. The richer our vocabulary, the better able we are to organize thoughts, to explain ideas, and to share knowledge. Words are an integral part of the very fabric of our lives. Words give texture, depth, organization, and perspective to the world in which we live.

Our lives, personal and professional, are dominated by words....

The approach to teaching vocabulary used in ***Open Court Reading*** reflects the belief that whatever system we use to organize our thinking needs to be approached explicitly, systematically, and continually. If children are to become fluent, confident, and enthusiastic readers—readers who easily gain meaning, pleasure, and knowledge from a variety of print materials—they need extensive experience with language and literature plus instruction in the skills necessary for accessing meaning in print. The building of a strong broad-based vocabulary is primary to this goal.

What Is Vocabulary and Why Is It Important?

Vocabulary is the sum of the words used by, understood by, or at the command of a person.

A Tool for Thinking

Development of vocabulary is important for several reasons. First, vocabulary is a tool for thinking. Baker et al. (1998a) note that without vocabulary, students are limited in their ability to restructure familiar concepts into new or novel combinations. The world we live in today is changing rapidly, and knowledge doubles every two years. With the transformation of the United States into a "knowledge society" (Drucker, 1993, as cited in Baker, Simmons, and Kame'enui, 1998), students need to be prepared to deal with increasing amounts of written information in increasingly complex ways. In order to do this, students must have the necessary skills. One critical tool for constructing meaning and delivering information is vocabulary knowledge—the ability to access the meaning of words quickly and efficiently, to think about how these words impact what we already know, and to add new knowledge and insight to our prior understanding.

Biemiller calls vocabulary the missing link between phonics and comprehension.

Successful Comprehension

Second, vocabulary knowledge directly affects successful comprehension (Beck, McKeown, and Omanson, 1987; Stahl, 1999). Much research shows that a strong relationship exists between vocabulary and comprehension. Readers who comprehend text well have extensive vocabularies (Anderson and Freebody, 1981; Nagy, Anderson, and Herman, 1987). Good readers can access the meaning of words rapidly and automatically in order to make sense of text. Improving student vocabulary impacts reading comprehension (McKeown, et al. 1983; 1985). This makes sense, yet meaningful, purposeful vocabulary instruction often appears tangential rather than integral to comprehension instruction.

Recent scores from the National Assessment of Educational Progress (NAEP) show that 37 percent of students read below the basic level, 31 percent read at the basic level, and only 24 percent were at the proficient level. The NAEP test is given in fourth grade, as students are just beginning to deal with text that has increased vocabulary and conceptual loads. Many factors affect student performance on comprehension measures. One cannot help but wonder how students' limited vocabulary or their lack of understanding about how to deal with unknown words will affect their performance on comprehension measures such as these, especially measures requiring the reader to make inferences and deal with content-specific text. The inability to infer the meaning of key words from context or to use structural elements to figure out word meaning does appear to have a significant impact on comprehension.

Foundation for Success

Finally, the lack of vocabulary development in the early years appears to have direct impact on children's later success in learning to read. Limited vocabulary knowledge affects successful reading even if students have learned how to read accurately and fluently (Becker, 1977; Chall et al. 1991).

When Should Vocabulary Instruction Begin?

Vocabulary development begins long before children ever enter school. Family members serve as children's first vocabulary teachers. Children have varied experiences in learning new words. While there is remarkable consistency in how children learn words and the order in which they learn words, large differences exist in the number of words children know when they come to school. The school's role in teaching vocabulary should begin the day children enter school. Education cannot control the different learning experiences before children come to school, but it can make a difference once children enter school. Biemiller (2000) notes that while all children might not have the same opportunities to learn new words, the research indicates that "children can acquire and retain two to three words in a day through instruction involving contextualized introduction and explanation of new words" (p. 29).

Kindergarten

Vocabulary instruction can and should be taught as early as kindergarten. When children first come to school, they have a fairly large listening and speaking vocabulary. According to Beck and McKeown (1991), the range of this speaking vocabulary is somewhere between 2,500 and 5,000 words. By first grade, many students have a speaking and listening vocabulary of about 6,000 words (Chall, 1987). From second grade on, vocabulary is no longer typically defined in terms of speaking and listening, but in terms of words understood and used in reading and writing. Graves, Juel, and Graves (1998) estimate that by the end of second grade, students' reading vocabularies range between 2,000 and 5,000 words. This vocabulary growth continues through the years, with typical readers increasing their vocabulary by an average of 3,000 to 4,000 words per year (Nagy and Anderson, 1984; Nagy and Herman, 1987). Given these growth figures and the limited amount of vocabulary formally taught in school, the assumption is often made that students acquire the bulk of new vocabulary primarily through implicit learning while reading. However, basing any instruction on assumption is chancy. Basing instruction in areas as crucial as vocabulary development on assumption can be disastrous.

From second grade on, vocabulary is no longer typically defined in terms of speaking and listening, but in terms of words understood and used in reading and writing.

The need to teach vocabulary beginning in kindergarten is made compelling by the fact that those students who have larger vocabularies upon entering kindergarten do better in acquiring new words than those with smaller vocabularies. This means that as early as kindergarten, a vocabulary gap begins. As Adams (1990) has noted, "We can directly access the meanings of only the words we already know. The referents of new words can be verbally explained only in terms of old words. This can be done either explicitly, by presenting their definitions, or implicitly, by setting them in a context of old words that effectively constrain their meaning" (p. 205). It appears critical that a primary responsibility of school is to help children, from the outset, develop vocabulary so they have a solid foundation for expanding their understanding and use of words to get meaning from text and to give them the base for learning new words.

Basing any instruction on assumption is chancy. Basing instruction in areas as crucial as vocabulary development on assumption can be disastrous.

Open Court Reading supports vocabulary instruction beginning at the kindergarten level as children experience well-written stories and expository text that introduce new words and concepts. Children are pretaught key words, experience these words, talk about the meaning of new words during reading, and use words in classification activities, writing, and discussion after reading. There is a continued emphasis on vocabulary learning throughout the ***Open Court Reading*** program.

***Open Court Reading* supports vocabulary instruction beginning at the kindergarten level.**

What Vocabulary Should Be Taught?

Not all unfamiliar words in a selection need to be pretaught. If the word is not critical for understanding the important ideas in the text, there is no reason to preteach the word. If the word is an example of a class or category that students know, then this word can be clarified during reading. In a selection entitled "Urban Roosts," it is very obvious that *killdeer* and *peregrine falcon* are types of birds. Having a deep understanding of these birds is not as important as understanding how they adapt to living in the city. Because the reader can quickly connect these unfamiliar words to a familiar concept, preteaching these words is not necessary or especially beneficial. In addition, it may not be important to preteach words that are clearly defined in the text. Stopping while reading to discuss and clarify the meaning of the word may be a more valuable learning opportunity than preteaching it.

Words that should be pretaught are those that are necessary for understanding the significant ideas in the selection, words that have the potential for appearing frequently in text, or words that support generalized learning—for example, words with Greek or Latin roots (Graves, Juel, and Graves, 1998).

Necessary for Understanding

Words necessary for understanding important ideas in text may be new words or words that are used in a unique or different context. Learning a new usage deepens students' understanding of an already familiar word and helps them appreciate the versatility of words. For example, in a selection on protective coloration, it is important to teach and understand the meaning of the word *camouflage* as it relates to animals. *Camouflage* is more than just protective coloration, which is what most students associate with the word since they may be familiar with camouflage suits worn by hunters or military personnel. In this case, the understanding of the word *camouflage* needs to be expanded beyond color to include shape and form.

Frequently Appearing Words

In the same context, a word such as *environment* may have specific references to animal camouflage and be used to some degree. A word such as *environment,* though frequently used in a specific text, is a very commonly used general term. The references to the environment and environmental concerns are numerous and encompass many different areas. It would be hard to read a daily paper without encountering the word *environment* in one or more of its forms. Therefore, explicitly teaching this word will serve not only to help in understanding the specific piece of writing but will add a widely used word to the students' vocabulary.

Greek and Latin Roots

While words with Greek and Latin roots are often related to specialized vocabulary, preteaching words with commonly used roots provides an instructional opportunity for teaching how a root can combine with different affixes to create new words with related meanings. If a word such as *aquarium* appears in a selection, it might make sense to preteach it even though it is not a word critical to understanding the main points in the text. The Latin root *aqua*, meaning "water", is found in a number of words: *aquarium*, *aquatic*, *aqueduct*, *aquifer*, *aqueous*, and *Aquarius*. Teaching *aquarium* as a means of understanding other words gives students useful, generalizable information. The same is true for Greek roots. *Aero* means "air" and is found in words such as *aerodynamics*, *aeronautical*, *aeroplane (airplane)*, and *aerosol*. Instruction of this type usually begins around fourth grade as students begin to encounter words with Greek or Latin roots in content area reading.

How Should Vocabulary Be Taught?

Unfortunately, there is no clear direction as to what is the most effective way to teach vocabulary. Nagy (1988) discusses two basic reasons for the failure of most vocabulary instruction. First, most vocabulary instruction does not produce sufficient in-depth knowledge to support comprehension. Second, the texts that students read do not support vocabulary growth. In general, texts seem to have sufficient redundancy so that the reader does not need to understand or know every word in the text to comprehend its meaning. While Nagy and Anderson (1984) have suggested that much of vocabulary development is a direct outcome of reading, if the text does not create sufficient demands on the reader to learn and use the vocabulary, then there may be less incidental learning of new words than is thought.

An analysis of reading texts by Chall and Conrad (1991) found the vocabulary load in reading programs to be less demanding than the vocabulary load in content-area text. Similarly, Stotsky (1997) noted the limited nature and scope of reading vocabulary in most contemporary reading series. If in fact one accepts the basic premise that word knowledge—vocabulary—is a tool to support thinking and organizing ideas, most reading programs do not provide sufficient opportunities to develop this critical tool in the context of reading.

In reviewing the body of work on teaching vocabulary, one will note the wide ranges of teaching techniques and activities, from semantic mapping to word webs to feature analysis to key-word techniques. In examining all these different methods for teaching vocabulary, one can see that they share some common principles. All of these methods

- work with the known to develop the unknown.
- get students involved.
- make vocabulary learning a thinking activity.
- provide multiple opportunities for students to use the words.
- use both contextual and definitional information.

Reading Aloud and Rereading

Reading stories with interesting and unfamiliar words does make a difference (Robbins and Ehri, 1994). Robbins and Ehri found that children were able to recognize the meanings of vocabulary words after listening to a story twice and hearing unfamiliar words repeated in the text of the story. Children who had larger vocabularies when they entered school made greater gains. Some implications for instruction follow. While reading to children in kindergarten is a very familiar activity, reading aloud at the upper grades is not as common. Evidence seems to support the notion of reading aloud to students of all ages. Selecting stories that stretch children's oral vocabulary is also important. This may mean including the reading aloud of not only fiction but nonfiction so students have the opportunity to experience technical as well as literate words.

Rereading stories also appears to strengthen vocabulary understanding.

Rereading stories also appears to strengthen vocabulary understanding. Interestingly, rereading is a strategy many readers naturally use to develop deeper understanding of text. Similarly, repeated readings of stories in kindergarten seem to help kindergarteners solidify their understanding of new words.

Active Involvement

Students need to be involved in learning about words. They need to think about words, figure out what a word means, and substitute new definitions in sentences. Students need to think not just about what the word means but what a functional definition might be, how the word is used, and how the word is connected to others they know. Having students involved with creating functional definitions as opposed to teachers giving definitions appears to be useful for learning new words.

Definition and Context

Learning new words can involve both definitional and contextual information. Students learn new vocabulary better when they receive and develop information beyond the definition level. Dictionary definitions pose many problems. First, there are often multiple definitions for a word, and unless students truly understand the context, they often go to the first definition, which may or may not be the best one. Second, many dictionary definitions require knowledge of the meaning of the word in order to understand the actual definition. In looking up the word *camouflage,* four definitions as a noun and two as a verb appear. The verb definitions require that a reader understand the noun definitions. The noun definitions use such words and phrases as *act or technique of disguising…, a device or stratagem for concealment,* and *the constructing of decoy objects….* The development of a functional definition created by students seems to be much more valuable and much more specific to the actual use of the word in the text. *Camouflage,* then, could be defined as the ability of animals to change color or form in order to protect themselves from other animals that may want to harm them.

Full Understanding

Students need to understand the how and the why of words. Connecting newly learned words to synonyms and antonyms (when appropriate), developing examples to achieve deeper understanding, or rewriting dictionary definitions as functional definitions helps learners connect the new word to something they already know or to transform the definitional information into useful information.

Multiple Exposure

Students need multiple exposures to words. Multiple exposures can occur through different learning experiences. Obviously this should be done through reading. Students should have multiple opportunities to encounter target vocabulary in text. Sometimes this is easily achievable. For example, in a unit on animal camouflage, students could encounter the word *camouflage* multiple times across different selections. Each time the word is encountered in text, however, readers can achieve deeper understanding as they learn that camouflage is not just about an animal concealing itself through protective coloration, but through changes in form and through mimicry as well. Consequently, understanding of the word *camouflage* deepens with each encounter. However, not all vocabulary words are encountered this way. Often the word may be used only one or two times in text in a grade level, so additional experiences need to be created. Preteaching vocabulary words, using vocabulary words during discussion and for writing, posting and revisiting vocabulary words on a regular basis, and making vocabulary words a part of a personal dictionary that students can refer to throughout the year will give students multiple exposures to new words.

Students need multiple exposures to words.

Manipulating Words

In addition, Beck, McKeown, and Omanson (1987) recommend that vocabulary instruction involve students manipulating words in "varied and rich ways." Discussing, manipulating, and connecting words to familiar words and experiences are essential to "rich instruction."

Explicit vs. Implicit

The question still remains—how should these instructional principles be applied to instruction? Should vocabulary be taught explicitly or implicitly or be some combination of the two?

Explicit Explicit vocabulary instruction often involves no more than giving students definitions or features of the words. In most programs, this instruction is done prior to reading with a goal that students will learn the words to a sufficient degree so that when they encounter these words during the actual reading, they will understand the words with a limited amount of effort, and comprehension will be assured. As any teacher knows, this is often not the case. Even with the most comprehensive preteaching, students may not remember the meaning of some of the eight to ten key pretaught words when they encounter the words in the actual text.

Explicit instruction needs to be expanded beyond this superficial level if students are to acquire a deeper understanding of new words in order to use and apply them to understand text, share ideas, and learn. Students need to understand words, where they come from, how they are used, and how they connect to words in their current repertoire. They need direct

explanation or modeling of how to figure out the meaning of new words. Just as comprehension strategies are modeled with think-alouds, this same overt thinking can be applied to vocabulary learning.

Implicit Implicit instruction presumes that students will infer the meaning of words as they are reading. Wide reading is considered critical. In many cases so much redundancy appears in text that the reader does not have to know the meaning of unfamiliar words in order to understand the text. When readers encounter a difficult word, they often skip the word, particularly if they are poorer readers. The implicit approach also assumes a certain base level of vocabulary knowledge that the reader can connect with in order to make sense of new words and more complex concepts. For students who do not have this base, learning words implicitly from text proves problematic.

What Are the Strategies We Need to Teach Students?

Kame'enui and Carnine (1998) talk about the need for "conspicuous strategies" as a critical part of an instructional program. "Extensive empirical evidence suggests strongly that all students in general, and diverse learners in particular, benefit from having good strategies made conspicuous for them, as long as great care is taken to ensure that the strategies are designed to result in widely transferable knowledge of their application" (p. 9). Teaching vocabulary is important, but teaching students explicitly how to figure out new words as they are reading appears to be more valuable. Students need to learn how to use skills and strategies and then learn to use those strategies independently through carefully scaffolded instruction.

Several different strategies for teaching vocabulary exist, including using definitions, context, and structural elements. Each can be taught explicitly to students.

Definitions There appear to be conflicting results on using definitions to teach students new vocabulary. Pressley and Woloshyn (1995) present research that supports the use of definitions to teach word meaning. However, Stahl (1999), suggests that teaching definitions by themselves appears to have little value for developing vocabulary. While students may use this technique to study for a test, there is little indication that students gain any useful generalized learning over time. The nature of the definitions themselves, however, may affect the use of definitions to teach new words. As noted earlier, dictionary definitions are often confusing and may use unfamiliar words to define the unknown word. McKeown (1993) found definitions with functional information and examples more valuable than dictionary definitions. Stahl (1999) has also discussed the importance of functional definitions for learning new words.

Teaching vocabulary is important, but teaching students explicitly how to figure out new words as they are reading appears to be more valuable.

Context Context is the environment in which words occur. The context, or the words and sentences surrounding an unfamiliar word, give the reader clues as to the meaning of the word. Because most readers seem to use context as the primary mode for figuring out the meaning of new words, it seems that explicit instruction in using context has value for teaching students how to learn new words. While context seems to be a very viable learning tool, it has its limitations. Sometimes the context itself contains unfamiliar words, the understanding of which is critical for figuring out the target word. This often occurs in content area text. Sometimes there is insufficient information for figuring out the target word. This is where context and structure may work together to give an unfamiliar word some meaning. Teaching students not only how but when to use context is critical.

Teaching students not only how but when to use context is critical.

Stahl and Shield (1992) reviewed a number of different approaches for teaching word meaning from context and noted four common elements that appear to impact the learning of new words.

- Teaching how to access the meaning of words through context appears to be more effective when it is taught as a strategy and not as a set of mechanical rules.
- Direct instruction of procedures supports vocabulary development.
- Students are given the opportunity to practice.
- The instruction motivates students to learn more about words. Success appears to breed success.

Teaching word structure and the meaning of some affixes and roots is a very effective way to foster vocabulary development.

Apposition Apposition, or definitions provided within the text itself, is a form of context and is often found in content-area text. While apposition seems to be so obvious that it almost does not merit instruction, many students read past the appositive statement without recognizing its role.

Word Structure Word structure requires the decomposition of a word into meaningful parts—affixes and suffixes. Teaching word structure and the meaning of some affixes and roots is a very effective way to foster vocabulary development. Biemiller (2000) suggests that learning new vocabulary can be made more manageable if we focus on root words rather than on the inflectional forms. If Biemiller is correct, and students acquire about 600 root-word meanings a year, many of which are similar in meaning, then vocabulary instruction becomes more clearly defined and manageable. By learning roots and affixes, students build a body of knowledge from which they can draw when they encounter unfamiliar words during reading. Rather than being intimidated by long words, they have a strategy to figure out the meaning of the word. Adams (1990) suggests that focusing on word parts such as affixes and roots reduces the size of an intimidating word and allows students to focus on relevant information within the word.

By learning roots and affixes, students build a body of knowledge from which they can draw when they encounter unfamiliar words during reading.

Prefixes are small, meaningful units added to the beginning of a base word or root that contribute to the meaning of a word. White, Sowell, and Yanagihara (1989) note that only 20 common prefixes account for 97 percent of the words with prefixes found in school English. Teaching the top nine to third graders along with a strategy for breaking words into parts—roots and affixes—appears to support word learning. The prefixes *un-* (not), *re-* (again), *in-* (not), and *dis-* (not or away) are used in 65 percent of words with prefixes (Honig et al., 2000). Teaching these four key prefixes appears manageable and useful.

Suffixes are meaningful units added to the end of words. Suffixes, such as the common inflectional endings *-ing*, *-ed*, *-s*, and *-es*, are found in most children's oral language and are usually understood when encountered in reading. These inflectional endings make up 65 percent of the most frequent suffixes found in printed school English (White, Sowell, and Yanagihara, 1989). Children may not need direct instruction on the meaning of these suffixes, although they may need some instruction with spelling changes that occur when they add these endings to words.

Derivational suffixes, however, often need instruction. While prefixes seem reliable in their spelling and have unambiguous meanings, the definitional teaching of suffixes appears less reliable (Honig et al. 2000). It may be hard to isolate the root, and often spelling changes may result (e.g., *-ion*, *-tion*, *-sion*,*–ation*, and *–ition*). It may be useful, however, to teach the more consistent suffixes such as *-ful* and *-less* to show how suffixes, like prefixes, affect word meaning.

Root words can take two forms. The root may be an actual word with an added affix, such as *unimportant* or *national.* While a pronunciation change occurs when a suffix is added to *nation*, the word itself is clearly recognizable. In this situation, if the root is part of the students' vocabulary, they can readily identify both the root and the affix and begin to construct meaning. In other cases the root is less clear, as in the words *biology*, *aquatic*, or *chronicle.* In these instances, the root may not be part of the students' vocabulary. Many content area words have their roots in Greek and Latin. Stahl and Shield (1992) and Honig et al. (2000) suggest teaching commonly occurring Greek and Latin roots. Teaching these roots as families may be particularly valuable because it enables the student to appreciate that knowing a single root has implications for learning a number of words.

Roots

Greek	Latin
arche – a beginning – *archaeology, architecture*	**aequus** – equal – *equation, equator*
aero – air – *aerodynamics, airplane*	**anima** – spirit, breath – *animal, unanimous*
bio – life – *biography, amphibious*	**aqua** – water – *aquatic, aquarium*
chronos – time – *chronology, synchrony*	**audire** – to hear – *audition, auditorium*
geo – earth – *geography, geology*	**candere** – to shine – *candle, chandelier*
graph – write – *autograph, biography*	**caput** – head – *captain, capital*
helios – sun – *helium*	**cedere** – to come, to yield – *recess, decease*
hydris – water – *hydrogen, hydroelectric*	**credere** – to believe – *incredible, credence*
logos – to speak – *apology, dialogue*	**duo** – two – *dual, double, duplicate*
metron – a measure – *diameter, symmetry*	**finis** – end –*finish, finite, refine*
monos – single – *monarch, monopoly*	**gradi** – to step – *degree, gradual, grade*
morph – shape – *morphology, amorphous*	**gratus** – pleasing – *congratulate, agree, grateful*
pathos – suffering – *sympathy, apathy, pathetic*	**liber** – free – *liberal, library, liberty*
photo – light– *photography, photomagnetic*	**mirus** – wonderful – *admire, miracle, mirage*
theao – I see – *theater, theory*	**nocere** – to hurt – *innocent, obnoxious*
therm – heat– *thermometer, thermonuclear*	**portare** – to carry – *portable, export*
scribere – to write – *describe, scribble*	
rupt – break – *corrupt, rupture*	
terra – land, earth – *terrain, terrier, territory*	
vivere – to live – *revive, survive, vivid*	

For example, understanding that *chron* (Greek root) means "time" helps when the reader meets words such as *chronicle, chronology, chronological, chronic,* and *synchronize.* While many of the words derived from Greek and Latin roots may be specific to content-area learning, as in the case of the words derived from *chron,* many are also part of a general literate, not content-specific, vocabulary.

Other Sources

In addition to teaching about context and structural elements, students need to know that other resources are available to them. Both can be modeled or taught explicitly.

Ask In school, students read with each other. One of the real benefits of this is the potential for collaborative effort—for students to solve problems as they read. One of these is dealing with unknown words. As students come to unknown words, they can stop and use each other as resources. Stahl (1999) talked about the importance of student involvement and the discussion of new words as part of building word knowledge, yet students seldom engage in real discussion about a word. Stopping to ask about a word often results in the person who responds giving an example, explaining the meaning in functional terms, or making a connection to more familiar words. Other students begin to share their understanding and give additional examples. Discussion of a word deepens understanding. Encouraging the use of fellow students as a resource becomes yet another valuable opportunity for explicit instruction.

Dictionary Using the dictionary to figure out the meaning of an unfamiliar word is perhaps the least productive avenue. As any teacher knows, students may look up the word, read the first definition, and then never read on. In addition, many dictionary definitions are difficult to understand because they often make use of equally unfamiliar words to define the target word. Scott and Nagy (1997) note that teaching word meaning using a dictionary often leads only to a superficial understanding of a word and does not result in long-term learning of words. This is not to imply that teaching students how to use the dictionary is not useful. It is an important resource and as students become interested in words, they may actually use the dictionary to explore words and their origins.

While context, structure, apposition, dictionary use, and asking someone are discussed individually, the reality is that readers should use all of these strategies and skills flexibly as needed.

Self-Monitoring

Teaching students how to figure out the meaning of words is only the first step. Students need to understand how to use these skills strategically while reading and become responsible for their use. As they read, students need to stop when they come to an unfamiliar word, decide what they know and do not know about it, and then try to determine its meaning. Stopping is a critical beginning. As teachers, how many of us have seen students read an unfamilar word and never stop to reflect on the word and its impact on meaning?

Stop

The first step is getting students to stop! Once students have stopped, they need to pull from the repertoire of skills they have learned to figure out the meaning of the word. "Sparrows and finches don't migrate, so you can watch them at backyard feeders throughout the year, chirping and chattering as they pick up seeds." The sentence gives some clues to the meaning of the word *migrate*—these birds can be seen all year round; they do not leave the city. Interestingly, the more specific meaning of migrate—to move from one climate to another to ensure a food supply and breeding location—is not available from this context or any of the other surrounding context.

Clarify

Stopping to clarify a strategy developed as part of reciprocal teaching (Palincsar and Brown, 1984) can be explicitly taught through modeling, initially by the teacher. The teacher can conspicuously or overtly present thinking on how to clarify through think-alouds. For example, the teacher might say, "The word *camouflage* seems critical for understanding ideas being presented in what I've read so far. I can get some general idea that it is about protection, but if I go on to the next sentence, the author defines it precisely for me." Scaffolded learning continues as the teacher moves from doing all the thinking to sharing the thinking with the class. Now, instead of the teacher determining how to clarify and to develop the definition, the teacher prompts the student to stop, identify how to figure out the word, and then come up with a functional definition or an example. Gradually the teacher removes all the scaffolding, and the responsibility for clarifying—doing the "difficult" thinking—lies with the student.

Knowledge Rating Checklist

Simple ideas, such as the use of a "knowledge rating checklist" similar to the one Blachowicz (1986) developed, may be helpful for students to monitor their thinking as they stop to clarify vocabulary in connected text.

- ✓ Do I need to know the meaning of this word?
- ✓ What do I know about this word?
- ✓ Have I ever seen or heard it before?
- ✓ What clues does the author give that can help me figure it out?
- ✓ What information does the author include in the text to help me figure out the meaning?
- ✓ How is this like other words I know?
- ✓ How can I connect this to what I already know? What are familiar examples?
- ✓ What word parts do I know?
- ✓ How can I define this word?
- ✓ Can I substitute the meaning in the sentences and does it make sense?
- ✓ What else do I need to know about this word?

Using the example from "Urban Roost," students read about certain birds that are found in the city and that these particular birds do not migrate. Stopping to figure out what *migrate* means is important to understanding why some birds are found in the city all year round and others are not.

Students may ask what they already know about this word. If they live in certain areas of the country, they may see a relationship between *migrate* and migrant workers— *people* who travel to different places during different seasons because work is available. Students can apply this knowledge to figure out that birds that do not migrate do not travel during different seasons. Or, students may ask themselves if the author provides any clues or insight into what the word means. In the text, the author lets the reader know that sparrows and finches do not migrate and that they can be seen at backyard feeders throughout the year. Given what they know about *migrate* from connections to what they already know and information in the text, students should see whether they can define the word. Using a series of questions leads students to a deeper understanding of the word. Asking the question, "What does *migrate* mean?" often leads to simplified definitions; for example, birds fly to different places. But asking questions such as "How does this word help me develop a better understanding of the characteristics of these birds?" "Why do birds migrate?" and "How does understanding this word help me connect with other information I have about birds?" leads students to a deeper understanding of the word.

What Does Vocabulary Instruction Look Like in the Classroom?

Preparing to Read

Because the major purpose of vocabulary instruction in a reading program is to help students become fluent, knowledgeable readers, providing vocabulary instruction before reading a selection helps students to see the connection between the instruction and the application of that instruction.

Teaching vocabulary in the early grades is critical.

As noted earlier, teaching vocabulary in the early grades is critical. This vocabulary instruction can and should be integrated into beginning reading instruction in the first and second grades. As students are learning how to blend words, they should also learn to build their understanding of words and inflectional endings that affect the meaning of words. Through practice with blending words, students can also learn antonyms and synonyms. Not only should students blend words, but they should also discuss the words they have read (blended), talk about their meanings, and use the words in sentences.

The emphasis in the first part of a reading lesson should gradually shift across the grades from phonics to word knowledge—learning roots and affixes and building derived forms so students see the relationship among words with the same root. In the upper grades, words discussed in the first part of a lesson should directly relate to words in the actual reading selection and should be organized to teach pronunciation, spelling, and meaning connections. Knowing the meaning of a root and affixes equals knowing the meaning a derived form. For example, if a reader knows the meaning of *civil,* then the reader can use that knowledge to figure out the meaning of *civilized* or *civilization.* If the reader knows the meaning of *nation,* he or she can use that knowledge to figure out *national, nationality,* or *nationalism.* As with blending in the lower grades, word knowledge should include discussion about the words and what they mean.

Reading

Before reading a selection, key vocabulary words should be pretaught using context, structural analysis, and/or apposition. Early in the year, students learn through direct explanation what these skills are and how to use them to figure out the meaning of key vocabulary words. As the year progresses, students increasingly take responsibility for deciding when and how to use these skills as they think aloud to figure out the meaning of the words. Pretaught words should be selected based upon saliency to developing understanding of the selection, frequency, and utility. Not all unfamiliar words should be pretaught. Some unfamiliar words should be dealt with during reading.

In addition to pretaught vocabulary words, students should have the opportunity before reading to browse the text for unfamiliar words and phrases. Often during browsing, students identify words that may be problematic during reading. This provides a preview of words they will need to think about while reading—words they will need to stop and clarify during reading.

Monitoring and Clarifying is a strategy used to check understanding while reading. Students need to learn to monitor understanding as they read, and to stop and clarify when something does not make sense. This could be at the word, sentence, or extended-text level. It could include pictures, charts, or graphs. Clarifying while reading provides a perfect context for addressing words that were not pretaught—words that may be examples of familiar concepts such as *killdeer,* which is a type of bird, or *mandolin,* which is a type of instrument. Having a detailed understanding of these words may not be critical for making sense of the text, but students can easily connect words such as these to a familiar concept during reading.

After reading, students should revisit vocabulary words. They may choose to keep a log of new words. In addition, students should always be encouraged to connect new words with familiar words—to write synonyms and antonyms when appropriate, to note related words, and to write examples. In other words, students personalize the learning of new words based upon what they already know. Students should feel free to add to this personal dictionary whenever they are reading.

People effectively learn new words by relating them to words they already know.

Language Arts

Specific language arts instruction can develop vocabulary skills and strategies to build new vocabulary and secure vocabulary through word relationships.

Vocabulary Skills and Strategies

Word Relationships People effectively learn new words by relating them to words they already know. An understanding of different word relationships enables students to secure new vocabulary quickly and efficiently. Word relationships include:

- **Antonyms** Words with opposite or nearly opposite meanings. *(hot/cold)*
- **Synonyms** Words with similar meanings. *(cup, mug, glass)*
- **Multiple Meanings** Words that have more than one meaning. *(run, dressing, bowl)*
- **Shades of Meaning** Words that express degrees of a concept or quality. *(like, love, worship)*
- **Levels of Specificity** Words that describe at different levels of precision. *(living thing, plant, flower, daffodil)*
- **Analogies** Pairs of words that have the same relationship. *(ball is to baseball as puck is to hockey)*
- **Compound Words** Words comprised of two or more words. *(daylight)*
- **Homographs** Words that are spelled the same but have different meanings and come from different root words. *(bear, count)*
- **Homophones** Words that sound the same but have different spellings and meanings. *(mane/main, to/two/too)*
- **Base Word Families** Words that have the same base word. *(care, careless, careful, uncaring, carefree)*
- **Prefixes** An affix attached before a base word that changes the meaning of the word. *(misspell)*
- **Suffixes** An affix attached to the end of a base word that changes the meaning of the word. *(careless)*
- **Concept Vocabulary** Words that help develop understanding of a concept. *(space, sun, Earth, satellite, planet, asteroid)*
- **Classification and Categorization** Sorting words by related meanings. *(colors, shapes, animals, foods)*

Contextual Word Lists Teaching vocabulary in context is another way to secure understanding of unknown words. Grouping words by subject area, such as science, social studies, and math, or in catagories such as descriptive words, new words, and so on enables students to connect word meanings and build vocabulary understanding.

- **Figurative Language** Idioms, metaphors, similes, personification, puns, and novel meanings need to be specifically taught, especially for English-language learners.
- **Derivational Word Lists** Presenting groups of words derived from particular languages or with specific roots or affixes is an effective way to reinforce meanings and spellings of foreign words and word parts.

Teaching vocabulary in context is another way to secure understanding of unknown words.

Vocabulary Strategies for Unknown Words

Different strategies have been shown to be particularly effective for learning completely new words.

Key Word This strategy involves providing or having students create a mnemonic clue for unknown vocabulary. For example, the word *mole* is defined in chemistry as a "gram molecule." By relating *mole* to *molecule,* students have a key to the meaning of the word.

Definitions Copying a definition from a dictionary is somewhat effective in learning new vocabulary. Combining using the word in writing and speaking adds to the effectiveness of this strategy. Requiring students to explain a word or use it in a novel sentence helps to ensure that the meaning is understood.

Context Clues Students can learn any word from context, particularly with repeated exposure to the word in reading and listening. Without specific instruction in using context clues, however, students often ignore unknown words. Three types of context clues can be used:

- **Syntax** How a word is used in a sentence provides some clue to its meaning.
- **External Context Clues** Hints to a word's meaning may appear in the words, phrases, or sentences surrounding a word in text. Other known words in the text may be descriptive, provide a definition (apposition), be compared or contrasted, or be used synonymously in context. Modeling and teaching students to use context to infer a word's meaning can help to learn unknown words.

Word Structure Examining the affixes and roots of a word may provide some clue to its meaning. Knowing the meaning of at least part of the word can provide a clue to its meaning. (For example, *unenforceable* can be broken down into meaningful word parts.)

Modeling and teaching students to use context to infer a word's meaning can help in learning unknown words.

Semantic Mapping Having students create a semantic map of an unknown word after learning its definition helps them to learn it. Have students write the new word and then list in a map or web all words they can think of that are related to the word.

Semantic Feature Analysis A semantic feature analysis helps students compare and contrast similar types of words within a category to help learn unknown words. Have students chart, for example, the similarities and differences between different types of sports, including new vocabulary such as *lacrosse* and *cricket*.

Building Word Knowledge and Vocabulary in *Open Court Reading*

Open Court Reading recognizes that vocabulary learning, like all learning, is multidimensional and must begin early and systematically. Students need to learn a repertoire of skills for dealing with unfamiliar words and how to use those skills in the context of reading a wide range of different texts. The support in ***Open Court Reading*** for vocabulary development is comprehensive and integrated throughout the program. Explicit vocabulary instruction occurs throughout every part of the three-part ***Open Court Reading*** lesson: Preparing to Read, Reading & Responding, and Language Arts.

Open Court Reading recognizes that vocabulary learning, like all learning, is multidimensional and must begin early and systematically.

- A Read Aloud selection appears at the beginning of every unit at every grade level. Work by Robbins and Ehri (1994) discusses the value of reading aloud to develop vocabulary with kindergarten children. Reading aloud introduces students to unit concepts and fosters conceptual "hooks" upon which students can begin to think about vocabulary specific to the unit theme.

- The literature in ***Open Court Reading*** provides a natural vehicle for introducing and building new vocabulary. Selections have been carefully chosen not just for content but for the opportunity to experience and learn new words and concepts. The literature itself supports the learning of new words and the broadening of understanding of known words as well as an appreciation of language.
- Investigations and exploration form an integral part of ***Open Court Reading*** as students explore new ideas, develop conjectures, and investigate potential answers to their questions. Additional reading, discussing, thinking, and sharing ideas make this happen. Focused reading on an idea or concept ensures that students will have multiple experiences with already learned vocabulary, deepen their understanding of existing words, and learn new ones. Ongoing opportunities to use new words in discussions and presentations help to solidify the understanding of words.

Stotsky (1997) examined the "literate vocabulary" in popular basal reading series and suggests that real differences exist between the language in ***Open Court Reading*** selections and that in other reading programs. ***Open Court Reading*** had more literate words in the fourth and sixth grade anthology selections (the two levels Stotsky examined) than did the corresponding grade-level anthologies in the other basal programs. These differences impact vocabulary growth. She states that "systematic differences in vocabulary development—and, hence, in reading growth—may be taking place today, depending upon the reading series used. That is because the more literate words children learn each year, the larger the vocabulary base they have with which they can learn even more literate words the next year" (p. 282).

According to Nagy (1988), "the single most important thing a teacher can do to promote vocabulary is to increase students' volume of reading." Creating opportunities for "reading, reading, and more reading" is critical. At the core of ***Open Court Reading*** is the belief that the reading that students experience through ***Big Books*** and ***Anthologies*** is only the beginning. These reading experiences act as catalysts for asking questions, generating wonderings, and creating a desire to learn more, and more, and more.

Conclusion

Vocabulary instruction should be a cognitive activity during which students think about words, explore their meanings, and deepen their understanding. Studying words should enrich students and support their success as learners. This learning of words must begin early to overcome the enduring effects that limited word knowledge can have on the academic and personal success of our students.

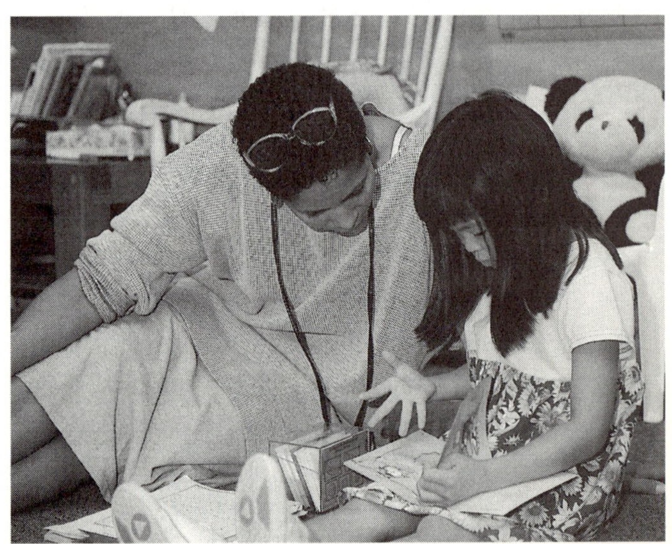

References

Adams, M. J. (1990). *Beginning to read: Thinking and learning about print.* Cambridge, MA: MIT Press.

Alllington, R. L. (1984). Content coverage and contextual reading in reading groups. *Journal of Reading Behavior, 16*, 85–95.

Anderson, R. C., and Freebody, P. (1981). Vocabulary knowledge. In *Comprehension and teaching: Research reviews*, J.T. Guthrie (Ed.), Newark, DE: International Reading Association, 77–117.

Anderson, R. C. and Nagy, W. E. (1991). Word meaning. In *Handbook of reading research* (Vol. 2), R. Barr, M. L. Kamil, P. B. Mosenthal, and P. D. Pearson (Eds.), White Plains, NY: Longman.

Baker, S. K., Simmons, E. C., and Kame'enui, E. J. (1998a). Vocabulary acquisition: Research Bases. In *What research tells us about children with diverse learning needs: Bases and basics*, Kame'enui, E. J. and Simmons, E. J. (Eds.), Mahwah, NJ: Lawrence Erlbaum Associates.

Baker, S.K., Simmons, E.C., and Kame'enui, E. J. (1998b). Vocabulary acquisition: Instructional and curricular basics and implications. In *What research tells us about children with diverse learning needs: Bases and basics*, Kame'enui, E. J. and Simmons, E. C. (Eds.), Mahwah, NJ: Lawrence Erlbaum Associates.

Beck, I. L. and McKeown, M. G. (1991). Conditions of vocabulary acquisition. In *Handbook of reading research* (Vol. 2), R. Barr, M. L. Kamil, P. B. Mosenthal, and P. D. Pearson (Eds.), White Plains, NY: Longman.

Beck, I. L., McKeown, M. G., and Omanson, R. C. (1987). The effects and uses of diverse vocabulary instructional techniques. In *The nature of vocabulary acquisition*, M. G. McKeown and M. E. Curtis (Eds.), Hillsdale, NJ: Lawrence Erlbaum Associates.

Becker, W. C. (1977). Teaching reading and language to the disadvantaged—What we have learned from field research. *Harvard Educational Review, 47*, 518–543.

Biemiller, A. (2000). Vocabulary: The missing link between phonics and comprehension. *Perspectives*, Fall, 27–30.

Biemiller, A. (1999). *Language and reading success.* Cambridge, MA: Brookline Books.

Blachowicz, C. L. Z. (1986). Making connections: Alternatives to the vocabulary notebook. *Journal of Reading, 29*, 643–649.

Blachowicz, C. L. Z. and Fisher, P. (1996). *Teaching vocabulary in all classrooms.* Englewood Cliffs, New Jersey: Prentice-Hall, Inc.

Chall, J. S. (1987). Two vocabularies for reading: Recognition and meaning. In *The nature of vocabulary acquisition*, M. G. McKeown and M. E. Curtis (Eds.). Mahwah, NJ: Lawrence Erlbaum Associates.

Chall, J. S. and Conrad, S. S. (1991). *Should textbooks challenge students?* New York: McGraw-Hill.

Chall, J. S., Jacobs, V. A., and Baldwin, L. E. (1990) The reading crisis: *Why poor children fall behind.* Cambridge, MA: Harvard University Press.

Graves, M. F., Juel, C., and Graves, B. B. (1998). *Teaching reading in the 21st century.* Boston, MA: Allyn and Bacon.

Honig, B., Diamond, L., and Gutlohn, L. (2000) *Teaching reading sourcebook for kindergarten through eighth grade.* Novato, CA; Arena Press.

Invernizzi, M. A., Abouzeid, M. P., and Bloodgood, J. W. (1997). Integrated word study: Spelling, grammar, and meaning in the language-arts classroom. *Language Arts, 74*, 185–192.

Kame'enui, E. J. and Carnine, D. W. (1998). *Effective teaching strategies that accommodate diverse learners*, Upper Saddle River, NJ: Merrill.

Lorge, I. and Chall, J. S. (1963). Estimating the size of vocabularies of children and adults: An analysis of methodological issues. *Journal of Experimental Education, 32 (2)*, 147–157.

McKeown, M. G. and Curtis, Mary E. (1987) *The nature of vocabulary acquisition.* Hillsdale, New Jersey: Lawrence Erlbaum Associates.

McKeown, M. G. (1993). Creating effective definitions for young word learners. *Reading Research Quarterly, 28*, 16–31.

McKeown, M. G., Beck, I. L., Omanson, R., and Perfetti, C. A. (1983). The effects of long-term vocabulary instruction of reading comprehension: A replication. *Journal of Reading Behavior*, *15*, 3–18.

McKeown, M. G., Beck, I. L., Omanson, R., and Pople, M. T. (1985). Some effects of the nature and frequency of vocabulary instruction on the knowledge and use of words. *Reading Research Quarterly, 20*, 522–535.

Nagy, W. E. (1988). *Teaching vocabulary to improve reading comprehension.* Newark, DE: International Reading Association.

Nagy, W. E. and Anderson, R. C. (1984). Learning word meanings from context during normal reading. *American Educational Research Journal, 24*, 237–270.

Nagy, W. E. and Herman, P. A. (1987). Breadth and depth of vocabulary knowledge: Implications for acquisition and instruction. In *The nature of vocabulary acquisition,* M. G. McKeown and M. E. Curtis (Eds.). Mahwah, NJ: Lawrence Erlbaum Associates.

National reading panel (2000). *Teaching children to read: An evidence-based assessment of scientific research literature on reading and its implications for reading instruction.*

Palincsar, A. S. and Brown, A. L. (1984). Reciprocal teaching of comprehension-fostering and monitoring activities. *Cognition and Instruction, 1*, 117–175.

Pressley, M. and Woloshyn, V (1995). *Cognitive strategy instruction* (Second Edition), Cambridge, MA: Brookline Books.

Robbins, C. and Ehri, L. C. (1994). Reading storybooks to kindergartners helps them learn new vocabulary words. *Journal of Educational Psychology, 86 (1)*, 54–64.

Scott, J. A. and Nagy, W. E. (1997). Understanding the definitions of unfamiliar verbs. *Reading Research Quarterly, 32*, 184–200.

Stahl, S. A. (1999). *Vocabulary development.* Cambridge, MA: Brookline Books.

References (continued)

Stahl, S. A. and Shield, T. G. (1992). Teaching meaning vocabulary: Productive approaches for poor readers. *Reading and Writing Quarterly: Overcoming Learning Disabilities, 8*, 223–241.

Stanovich, K. (1986). Matthew effects in reading: Some consequences of individual differences in the acquistion of literacy. *Reading Research Quarterly, 21*, 360–407.

Stotsky, S. (1997). Why today's multicultural readers may retard, not enhance, growth in reading. In *Readings on language and literacy* (L. R. Putnam, Ed.), Cambridge, MA: Brookline Books.

White, T. G., Sowell, J. and Yanagihara, A. (1989). Teaching elementary students to use word-part clues. *The Reading Teacher, 42*, 302–309.